For Aliya.
10.27.2016

# A Father's Choice.

# Contents

# Contents

# Before we do this thing

     First of all, thanks for picking up a copy of this book and giving it a shot. Whether you bought a copy or talked someone into lending it to you, I hope that it offers up some valuable insight and perspective, or if you are not in the same situation as me at least maybe some entertainment value. So again, thank you.

     What you are about to dive into is an accounting, from my perspective, of the first few challenges and struggles that I faced with my daughter. I wrote the draft for the bulk of it in a notebook over the course of about twenty days while I was on a training mission to Fort Hood, Texas in June 2017. I wrote it during what little blocks of down time I had, and as such it is done in sections in sort of a journal-style format, so if that bothers you or isn't what you were expecting, my apologies (but give it a shot anyway).

My daughter Aliya is eight months old at the time of this writing. She is the light of my life (as you will find out if you continue reading this); she is an energetic, sweet, and curious little thing. She was also born with Down syndrome. Obviously this presents some challenges, especially for a first time parent, and a father who has a habit of being socially distant with people naturally in the first place. I myself am an entrepreneur, a musician, a biker, a soldier, a gamer, and an all-around goofy individual. But above all of these things, now I am also a father, and as any first-time father would I have had to deal with that transition.

This will be an accounting of the decisions that I had to make early on, the challenges that went along with those decisions, and the early journey that I took with a beautiful little girl. I hope that it will serve to give some perspective to anyone who is also facing what I had to face, provide some reassurance, and help people understand that they are not alone regardless of what they are going through. If this book helps at least one person, gives perspective to at least one person, or even puts a smile on my little girl's face later in life, then it was worth writing.

# June 4th, 2017. Indecision.

Sitting here at the armory in Gallatin, TN. The unit is supposed to catch a flight this afternoon between 1600 and 1800 (which means probably a couple hours later than that) to Fort Hood for three weeks of absolute horse crap, better known as a training exercise. I have been in the Army (on the National Guard side) for six years now (which is crazy when I think about it), so I am used to this sort of thing by now. The biggest question weighing on my mind right now is "what do I really want to write about?"

For a while now I have felt the increasingly overwhelming need to start writing a book, and this time finish it (I've tried a time or two before and never followed through). For the life of me, however, I can't decide on a solid topic. There are a lot of experiences in my life that are worth writing about...at least to me...and maybe I'll get to them eventually. But which one is worth being the first? Which one would someone else get the most out of reading about most? My time in the military, the people I've met and friends I've had, places I've been, the travelling, the motorcycles I've ridden and where to, the games I've played, the guns I've shot, women that have come and gone (or not gone), my family with all of it's own craziness...or maybe all of the crazy experiences I've had playing music over the last decade plus. These are all worthwhile topics in my mind, but there's one that keeps coming back over and over again to the forefront. Aliya. My daughter Aliya, and just how special she truly is. So whether I decide to publish it or not, I think this one will be for her.

# Birth.

On October 27th, 2016, Aliya Gwendolyn Simmons came screaming into this world. Well she wasn't screaming at first, but a few seconds after she popped out the nursing staff woke her up, and she figured it out.

We had been at home the night before, and I was actually just getting ready to go to sleep when my girlfriend Mandy shook me awake. She had been having some discomfort all day, and finally had decided that we needed to go to the hospital. I was still half asleep, so I replied something to the effect of "nah, you'll be fine, just go to sleep and I'll take you in the morning if you need to go." I know, I know...boyfriend of the year award right? So she shakes me again and says "seriously, I think I'm having labor pains and we need to go to the hospital." Not being enthusiastic about this at all, I rolled out of bed, pulled my jeans on, and said "ok, ok, fine. Get dressed, grab your bag, and get in the truck." She did just that, and at around 10:30pm we drove the twenty minutes down to Centennial Children's Hospital in Nashville, where she was already set up to have this baby.

We had been to Centennial several times already for Mandy's check-ups, so I already knew where to go, where to park, and where the Children's ER was, which are all handy things when you're dealing with angry pregnant lady. When I took Mandy inside and we got her checked in, the nurse at the desk proceeded to tell me that I would have to wait in the lobby. I asked the lady very politely "who exactly intends to stop me from going back there with her?" She simply restated that I had to wait, that it was hospital policy and there was nothing she could do about that. I told her, again very politely, that they had twenty minutes to get her settled and do what they had to do, then I was coming back whether they liked it or not. Thankfully for all parties concerned they came out in exactly twenty minutes, and took me back to Mandy's delivery prep room. Fast forward several hours worth of labor (Dad showed up at some point to help keep me from going crazy), and Mandy delivered at eight-something the next morning (October 27th, but I'm sure Mandy will want to kill me for not knowing the exact time. I suck at that).

Over the years, I have sort of developed a reputation for being a non-emotional hard-ass. When they took that little girl from the delivery doctor over to a side table to get her measurements, and asked me to come stand there while they did so, I thought I was looking at a little pale hairless pygmy alien that was raising absolute hell and just refused to settle down. Then she grabbed my pinky finger and stopped crying, and at that point I knew that I was hopelessly in trouble.

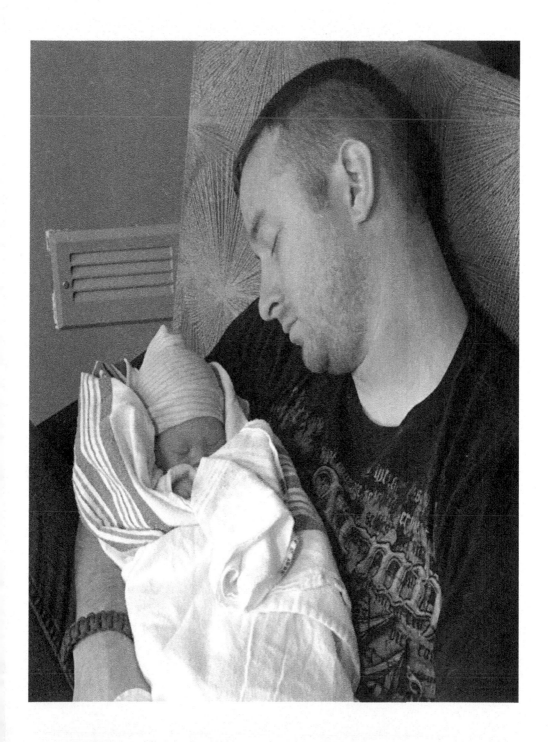

# Finding Out.

I will never forget the day that we found out. Not that we were going to have a baby, Mandy found that out in the early Spring of that year and told me when I returned home from a short Army trip to Fort Campbell. And not that we were having a girl, that was another visit altogether, and not-so-shocking since that was a 50-50 shot anyway. The day during Mandy's pregnancy that will always stick out clearest in my mind is the day that we were told that our child would have a little something extra that would change our lives forever, even more so than having our first child already would.

It started like any other OBGYN visit day (going to the pregnancy doctor). I can't remember the exact date (which once again I am sure Mandy will kill me for when she reads this), but it was sometime in the summer. We always had these appointments on Tuesdays or Wednesdays because in my line of work you get Sunday off plus a weekday, which can rotate based on customer volume. Like any other of those day-off appointments we got up that morning, got ready, and drove that familiar twenty minutes to Centennial Medical Plaza to see her OBGYN, who for the sake of privacy we will call Dr. W. This was actually my first visit to see Dr. W. with her, she always wanted me to go but I had been unable to up to that point (which is why we changed it to my days off).

Now before we go on I have to admit that at first I did not care much for Dr. W., but this turned out to be entirely unfair. It was purely due to the news that he was unfortunately obligated to deliver to us the first time that I met the man. As it would turn out he was a kind, well-mannered, professional, and extremely competent doctor. He did a great job with Mandy's pre-natal care as well as the delivery, no complaints here, just for the record. The majority of this visit went fine; they took Mandy's vitals which were fine, listened for the baby's heartbeat, that was all fine too. Then Dr. W. comes in and tells both of us that he has the results back from early preliminary testing. In a very flat and matter-of-fact tone, he gave us the news. (As I am writing this I've just flipped a page in this notebook to find "Aliya and I love you" scribbled into the middle of the next page. Could not have come at a better time.)

The Doctor told us that our unborn child has tested positive for Trisomy twenty-one, better know as Down Syndrome, with results being about ninety-eight percent accurate. It took a moment for me to really process what he was saying, and then he reiterated again "your baby will have Down Syndrome." Of course we couldn't truly even process what this meant for us yet, not fully, we were both in a strange state of polite shock. Dr. W. of course was somewhat used to this effect, and offered up some usual explanations of "there will be no way to tell what the severity of this will be yet, but most of these kids end up leading fairly normal lives." He then rattled off the long list of typical physical defects we needed to be prepared for, highest on the list being heart-related issues. Mental delays of course were to be expected, the degrees of which were also uncertain, as well as a laundry list of other possible issues. He told us that our probability of this had been higher due to Mandy's age at the time, that the risk and occurrence of Down Syndrome was increasingly common in later pregnancies with women. This was all great useful info, but he had just dropped a bomb right on my head, and at the time I hated the man for it.

At that moment I wanted to rip that doctor's throat out. My first child would have Down Syndrome, and he was the man that had to tell me.

The last thing that he said to me was that we would need to decide whether we were keeping the baby or terminating the pregnancy, which brought forth a whole new tornado of internal emotional struggle for both of us. After that the visit wrapped up, and we left the doctor's office. As we took the elevator down to the parking garage, I did something that I had very seldom done before having a child. Without letting Mandy see it, I allowed a single tear to roll down my left cheek.

***

From the doctor's office to the truck my mind was racing. All I could think about was what had been said about making the decision to keep or not to keep. When my mind gets spun up and rolling on a topic, it's like a bullet train filled with molten lead barreling down a track at top speed with the brakes disconnected. There's no stopping it or slowing it down until it arrives at its destination...and even then good luck. I knew that ultimately, for whatever reason, Mandy would leave this decision up to me.

I was determined to make the right choice, whether it was for me out of pure selfishness, for Mandy's sake, for my family's, or for this baby that was still barely formed. At that point if I remember correctly we didn't even know if it would be a boy or girl, that's how early it was in the pregnancy (I think anyway). Yet I was left with the task of deciding whether or not this child, my child, would ever actually "be."

# Deciding.

Keep in mind that all of the mental turbulence that I am about to cover went through my head in the span of time between leaving the doctor's office, and getting into my truck in the parking garage. By the time we got in the truck and started driving, I gave Mandy my decision.

The first things to run through my mind of course were all of the stereotypical things that I had come to understand over the years about people with Down Syndrome. To be honest at that point I did not really know a lot, but what I did know led me to believe that it would cause a lot more difficulty throughout life for both the child and the parents. I knew that people with Down's were generally slower mentally, that they had some specific physical differences which made them easy to identify, and that they often had physical defects at birth that made them prone to medical issues as children if not also later in life. Since I had never personally been close enough to really know anyone with this extra chromosome (which is what Down Syndrome is, an extra chromosome), what I did NOT know at the time was that people with Down's also tend to be some of the most genuine and caring people you will ever know. For some reason their inability to get or comprehend many of society and/or life's little nuances also seems to free them from a lot of life's petty crap.

I also knew that as a father and sole household income provider, this would put an even greater strain on an already tight household budget with expected baby expenses. Special needs kids have more medical needs, extra doctor visits, often times require therapy, all of which were expensive propositions. Soon after the baby's due date my enlistment in the Army was due to be up, and I wanted very badly to get out. I had put in six years with the National Guard, figured my time had been served for my country, it was time for my weekends and summers to be mine again, and maybe I wouldn't have to use all of my vacation time from work every year shooting things for Uncle Sam anymore. But with the Army also went the good affordable health insurance...and decent family insurance plans on the private market were becoming an increasingly expensive unicorn (once again, the next page in my notebook has a cute message from the family).

Then there was simply my own ability to understand and handle this child. I am one of those people who already have issue connecting with most other people on a lot of levels because most people don't "get" me very easily. So how in the hell was I supposed to connect with a child, let alone a child with a disability that would make it harder for us to understand each other?

If I came to terms with all of those things, how would Mandy deal with this child if I DID reenlist, which would mean that I would be gone with my Army unit on a regular basis, leaving her home alone with a special needs child? What would happen if I had to deploy to a combat zone, or anywhere for that matter? How was she supposed to support and take care of this child if something happened to me? Without my income, let alone my insurance, how would they make ends meet, even before all of the therapies and extra medical help this child would need?

How was the rest of my family going to handle this? I would be the first of my generation in our family (between two brothers and myself) to have a kid. How were my mother, father, and grandmother going to react to their first grandchild having Down

Syndrome? They are all very accepting, caring, and understanding people, but I still didn't know how they would handle this either. As far as I knew we had never had a special-needs child in our family. I was sure that they would accept and love the child just as much if not more, but the question still ran around inside my head.

Needless to say for that short amount of time (from office to truck) I was a complete and utter mess. It hadn't really been very long since I had started coming to terms with having my first kid at all, which I swore as a young man I would never do (we are all sorts of stupid when we are young), and now I had this to deal with? What in the hell?

By the time we got down the elevator in the medical center building, across the third-floor skywalk breezeway, and through the parking garage to my truck, I had at least solidified my thoughts (well most of them, but I was still a mess in my head about some of it). I decided not to bring up my decision until Mandy did, so I could also feel out where she stood on all of this. After all she was the one that had to carry the baby, not me (I just had to put up with her while she did. I'm waiting for her to read this and come throw something at me). So I started the truck, we made the winding descent down to the ground level of the garage to the exit, and pulled out onto the side street that runs through the middle of Centennial medical plaza. Two quick right hand turns and one left, and we were headed home down what would turn into Clarksville pike. About half of the drive home went by in a relative silence. Then Mandy turned to me and said something to the effect of leaving the decision to me, meaning the to-keep-or-not-to-keep issue. I told her that as far as I was concerned we were keeping it, no doubt about it. Period.

***

As far as I was concerned, no matter what the issues or hardships it would cause, we were having the baby. Now I can remember that we definitely did not know the child's gender yet, because my boss called me later that day after I had texted to tell him that I needed a day or so off, and I remember in that conversation referring to "the baby" instead of "she" or "her." Over the course of the next day or so the news that we had received was spread throughout our network of family and friends, some by phone, others by the modern wonders of texting and Facebook. Sure as can be, the calls and texts started pouring in. They came from family, close and not-so-close. They came from friends, current and past. They came from acquaintances from every walk of my life, band members, other music contacts, Army buddies, and a ton from co-workers or professional contacts. They all called or texted to say that they had heard, that they were so sorry, that they couldn't imagine being in my shoes. I thought to myself that of course they couldn't imagine being in my shoes, this had happened to me, not them. But all I said to anyone was how much I appreciated it, that I appreciated all the concern, which I really did (though at the time I really didn't understand how much I appreciated it, because I couldn't process much beyond my own default coping mechanism, which is anger). What I did not understand yet, because I did not really understand my daughter's particular disability yet, was that all of these people really should not have been offering up such condolences. Everyone thought that this was such a bad thing that had happened to me. They thought in their minds, but not outwardly of course, that I had been cursed with this terrible burden. I could tell by tone, demeanor, and careful choice of words that this was the case. They were all inwardly glad that it wasn't them in these shoes, dealing with this situation. Theirs was a response of honest and heartfelt concern, combined with an inward relief that it wasn't them. The only exception being a couple of immediate family members, and another young couple that we are good friends with, Preston and Martha. They alone congratulated me on the opportunity that Mandy and I had been given, even though we did not yet understand it as such, to make a difference. As for the rest of my circle of concerned callers, I told them all the same thing...

I had decided that we would have this child. I was determined to take on the responsibility, and do what I needed to do to make it all work. My child deserved a chance, and I wasn't going to deny her that chance just because she wasn't perfect. She would get all of the opportunity that I could give her, and I would help her become every bit of who she could be. If she had a mild case of symptoms and characteristics, awesome. If she had a sever case and tons of issues, so be it, bring it on. I made the conscious decision that she would exist, and I would take care of her, teach her, help her, and above all else I would defend her from the world, the whole world and everyone in it if I had to.

Because I was her father damn it, and I dared the world to try to hurt my daughter.

# The ICU.

    The first day after Aliya's birth things went fairly smoothly, or at least they did based on my extremely limited understanding of how they should go when you've just had a baby. She and Mandy were admitted to the hospital, put in a room, and monitored to make sure things went right. Aliya was put in this crazy little crib/incubator thing to monitor and keep her warm. Everything was going fine for a while, so I went home to feed animals, walk the dogs, and get a little sleep. During that time Aliya was taken to do some basic tests, and apparently the nursing staff had a hard time finding her veins for a blood draw (due to her being small, 6lbs at birth, and having mottled skin as Down's babies tend to have). Somewhere in that mess she was uncovered for a little too long, and her temp dropped a couple degrees below where the staff was comfortable with it, which in that hospital's policy means and automatic trip to the NICU (neonatal intensive care unit, baby ICU).

Needless to say this sent me in a tailspin of being both concerned, and outright pissed off. I went into an immediate rampage of wanting to know who had screwed up such a simple thing as a blood draw, and landed MY daughter in the ICU. I wanted to know how she was doing, and when we could get her back out of there. Luckily my father had already been there, and my mother drove up that first night from Florida (A.K.A. home, A.K.A. paradise), and between the two of them I was given some perspective, calmed down, and talked off the ledge. This was good, because I was about ready to kill every set of scrubs that I could get my hands on. And so it went that Mandy got a hospital room, and our daughter got an ICU incubator.

The first thing I did was go to see her, as soon as I was able to of course. She was in a NICU holding area (later that day they put her in a regular NICU "cubicle"), which we had to go through a five minute scrub-in process to get access to every time. We played this game several times a day while she was in the NICU, since I had to keep running home and back to take care of things there. Even after Mandy was discharged from the hospital I let her stay there with Aliya while I ran back and forth so that she could have twenty-four hour access to our daughter.

That first time in the ICU that I saw my newborn daughter covered in monitor wires, IV lines, and laying under a heat lamp, I almost swallowed my own throat. She was tiny, I could easily hold her whole upper half in one hand, and that heat lamp crib thing made her look even smaller. She had good nurses in there at least, which I guess I should have expected in a newborn ICU. They were polite and competent, which made one of my earliest interactions with them very, very unfortunate.

During that first visit with Aliya in the ICU she was asleep, breathing normally (they had stopped giving her oxygen very soon after putting her in the ICU since she didn't need it), and everything seemed to be going fine with her. I think I remember the nurse telling me that they had just finished feeding her. I can remember putting my right hand in the incubator crib and next to hers, even though she was sleeping. I guess maybe I thought it would be reassuring, thought I doubt she knew I was even there. Then she grabbed hold of my infantry school ring and held it for a minute or so, which damn near broke my heart and gave me an idea. I took my ring off and set it on her chest, then reached in my pocket for my iPhone. Now, one of the

NICU rules that we were told about was not to take things out of our pockets once we were scrubbed in...and they really didn't want us playing with our cell phones in there at all. I thought to myself however that my daughter was not there for any sort of post-op recovery, and I didn't see any sort of infection risk, so I just went for it.

As soon as the iPhone was out of my pocket, as if right on cue, a nurse came swooping out of nowhere and asked me to put it away. I said that I was "just going to snap a picture real quick," and carried on. Her courteous response was simply "you can't do that in here." At that point unfortunately (in hindsight), my dad mode kicked in, and I answered her with an authoritatively-toned question of "and exactly which of you intends to stop me?" She looked a little flustered, but did not protest further. I snapped my picture, put my phone back in my pocket, and my ring back on my finger.

I came to visit often during Aliya's initial stay in the hospital, but due to a couple of unfortunate little interactions like the one I just described, I didn't stay too long per visit. Between taking care of the animals etc. at home, handling my job, and my personality clashes with hospital staff (yay type A dominant...), I decided it best to let Mandy be the always-there parent. She was much nicer and more even-tempered with the medical staff anyway, whom for whatever reason I have always had a tendency to get a little bit sideways with.

As soon as I left the NICU that day I pulled my phone back out of my pocket, and pulled up the all-too-popular Facebook app. I posted a picture to my timeline of my baby girl laying there in the ICU, wires and monitors and all, and my infantry ring from my time at Fort Benning resting on her little newborn chest. The caption for the picture read as "protected by daddy."

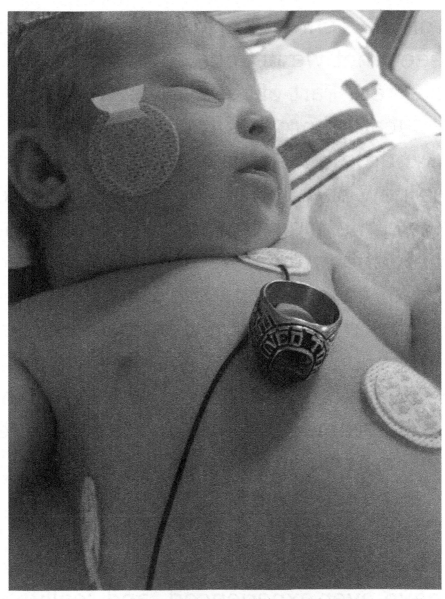

During that initial hospital stay my
mother had also contacted the local
Down Syndrome network there in

middle Tennessee to get some info and see what we needed to do to get started. Part of the welcoming and education process for the Down Syndrome network was an initial visit to new parent at the hospital, just to welcome them to the community and help them understand what to expect. So of course being the woman that she is, my mother went ahead and set up just such a visit.

The lady that came to visit us there at Centennial was very nice, and she brought along her own little girl as well, a two-year-old that also had Down Syndrome. This little girl was one of the most encouraging things I have ever experienced, and really helped me to better understand what I could expect. Up to that point I had been doing a lot of reading up on Down Syndrome, particularly what to expect and what we would likely be dealing with as far as limitations. That two-year-old girl that visited us at the hospital shattered my expectations and filled me with hope (for the life of me I can't remember her name, and I'm not asking Mandy because she doesn't know I'm writing this book). She was nothing that I had expected at all. The only things she possessed that I had expected were the typical physical facial features like almond shaped eyes, and tongue that hadn't quite learned to stay behind its own teeth yet. Otherwise she was an energetic, physically active and decently coordinated, cute little girl. I am most thankful for the welcoming visit because it gave me that opportunity to meet her. We also received a nice little goodie bag of books and material to get us started along the journey. All in all it was a really cool little thing that the Down's network in TN does.

Aliya only spent a few days in the hospital that first time as a precaution, just to monitor and make sure she didn't have any preliminary issues. She held good temperature, ate adequately, and her vitals all stayed looking good. So after a few days, we took Aliya home to my little place in Joelton.

# Opening Eyes.

The first few days after Aliya came home for the first time weren't too exciting. Like any newborn she mostly slept. She slept all the time, and ate, and pooped, and then slept some more. We had previously set up a futon in the nursery room, which Mandy then insisted on sleeping on so she could be right there if Aliya needed anything. This was fine with me, since it let me get a little more sleep so I could get up and go to work every morning, but I told her she didn't have to, we did have baby monitors and her room was just down a hallway from ours. She still insisted though, she wasn't comfortable leaving her in there by herself yet, so obviously I wasn't going to argue the point much further.

It was really odd to me at first how reluctant Aliya was to open her eyes. In those early days she would sort of open them occasionally, but it was very rare and didn't typically last very long. She HAD been born about a week early, but at just over six pounds birth weight and not showing any signs of premature issues the doctor had deemed her plenty developed and fine to go home. Thus her refusal to open her eyes really confused her father for a while (yes that was a third person self referral). In fact she did not start really opening her eyes consistently or leaving them open for a few weeks after she came home, but once she did they were a pretty light blue...looked just like her father's (yep, there's myself in the third person again).

Another odd thing that happened early on was that once she started opening her eyes a lot and being aware of her surroundings, Aliya stopped eating very well. At that age and weight her pediatrician told us she expected her to eat about four ounces per feeding, but most of the time if she was awake it was hard to get more than two into her. Eventually we would figure out that she ate way better if she was half asleep and not alert, so for example if we waited for her to fall asleep and then fed her she would easily eat twice as much. There didn't seem to be much explanation for this, but it ended up being fixed later on when we fixed another issue, which we will get into shortly.

During these early weeks and first couple of months it was hard to get a good feel for what Aliya's personality would be like or how her syndrome would affect her. As far as we knew or could tell she was a typical baby. As I said before she ate, she pooped, and she slept a lot. We would play with her, she would laugh and smile, but she really did not play with toys at all, she didn't really cry unless something was really wrong, and she overall was very easy to deal with. We noticed she did love to be held, as I would guess any baby would, and she loved the ocean or creek noises we could play for her from this little crib sound box thing. At around that time I also read in several books that we needed to work with her to develop her arms and legs, as development of limb muscles was a common issue with Down's kids, so every day I would spend a little time playing with her and working those limbs out a little bit, moving them up and down, in and out, all around and back again.

During those first few months I had limited time to spend with Aliya while she was awake, so I split our time together between working with her limbs and taking walks around the house. She seemed to love those walks once her eyes were open. She would get crazy wide-eyed and look curiously at everything around her. Her expression would go from surprise, to happy, and back again. Though she didn't play with toys much early on, she loved to hold onto my fingers. Maybe this was a natural and common thing, or maybe it was a comforting instinct going back to that first time at the hospital. Either way she has always loved to hold my fingers or hand, and often when she has been upset it has been the fastest way for me to calm her down.

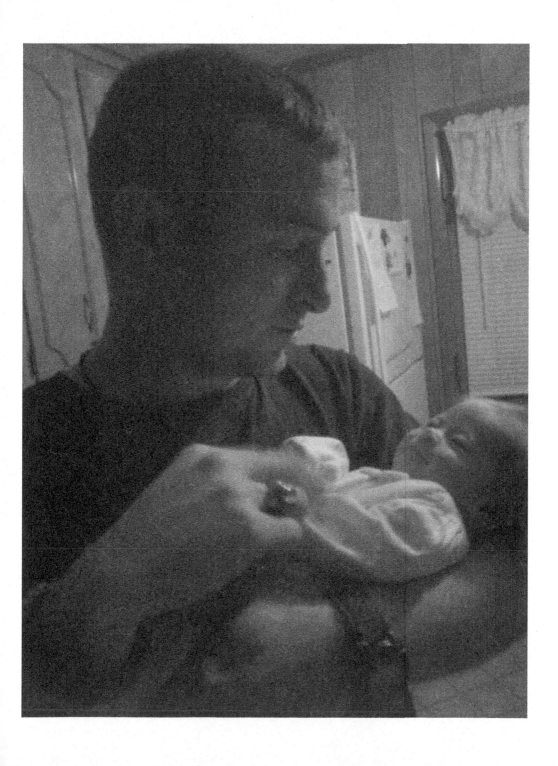

# Cardiology.

When Aliya was born the staff at
Centennial performed a heart echo on
her. Apparently this was done as a
standard precaution for all kids born
with Down Syndrome (maybe all kids
in general, but they said definitely for
kids with Down's). Well that echo
showed a very small septal defect in
her heart (a hole between two
chambers of her heart) that was
allowing a small amount of blood to
shunt between chambers inside her
heart. At the time it was small and not
concerning, so they were fine letting
her go home, and we were set up with
a top-notch pediatric cardiologist
(children's heart doctor for those that
don't know), for the purposes of this

book and privacy we will call him Dr. P., for follow up visits and monitoring the situation. Although Mandy was fine taking Aliya to pediatrician appointments just the two of them, she insisted on always trying to set up the cardiology visits so that I could go with them.

Dr. P.'s office was in a building directly across the street from Centennial Children's hospital, so conveniently I already knew the place, where to go, what garage to use, all that good stuff. It was the same song and dance of going up one elevator, across a skywalk, up another elevator, and down a hallway that we had done all along for her pregnancy visits. Familiar territory.

During these visits we would get checked in, a nurse would weigh and check Aliya's overall length, and then an echo technician would take us to a quiet dark little room to perform the actual echo pictures (as much as Aliya would cooperate for anyway). Then we would wait as the doc examined the pictures, read the echo, and made his determinations. It always seemed like an eternity, when in reality it didn't take the man very long at all...maybe forty-five minutes to do the echo and fifteen minutes to read the thing.

That first visit, after all of the song and dance that I just described was done, we had our first consultation with Dr. P. about what he saw on the echo. He examined Aliya and listened to her heart, then proceeded to discuss the echo with us and what the pictures actually meant. He confirmed that she did in fact have a septal defect in her heart, that it was relatively small, and at this early stage was not super concerning. He did want to keep an eye on it, stating that sometimes these types of holes would close on their own, other times the kids would need corrective surgery to fix them. In the meantime he wanted to prescribe her a diuretic lasiks, namely Furosemide, to help with blood flow and ease any strain or stress the internal shunting might cause on her heart. And that's how our first visit went, "we don't know if she will need surgery or not, take this medication and come see the doc again in two weeks."

So this was also surprisingly my first experience with prescriptions or pharmacies. I ironically had never had to order prescriptions up to this point. If I had ever been sick or injured I pretty much refused to go see a doctor, so it was either handled with over-the-counter type meds or whatever an ER gave me if it was bad enough. I am only mentioning this because I want to bring to your attention a major "up-yours" that I received from a major drugstore company as a result of this first experience with prescription medications.

When Dr. P. asked me which we would like to use for Aliya's meds, the first thing that came to mind was the closest one for me on my way home...CVS...just a few miles down Clarksville Pike from home...super easy and convenient, right? So the doc called it in, and on the way home I tried to be a good dad...I stopped in at my friendly (so I would have thought) local CVS to get my daughter's medicine. When I arrived at the prescription counter and asked the lady about Aliya's prescription being called in, she (the pharmacy lady) asked me to hold on just a second. After a very short minute she came back to me and explained that they could not fill my prescription, because I had insurance through the Army (Tricare), and CVS pharmacy had decided as a whole corporation not to accept military Tricare insurance any longer. Needless to say I was mildly stunned. The largest pharmacy chain in the United States no longer accepted Army insurance? Are you kidding me?

If anyone from CVS corporate is reading this, you should reconsider this course of action. By doing this, regardless of the reasoning which I am sure you have (maybe that particular insurance is slow to pay or something of that nature), you are successfully alienating hundreds of thousands of service members who bust and risk their butts every day for this insurance...and rely on it for their families. Just saying, think about it.

After that fiasco we got the prescription called back in with my next closest choice, good ole' Kroger, and I had zero issues getting it filled for her. To my surprise, she took her medicine like an absolute champ, no issues at all. I figured that as a baby, especially one that wasn't so good at eating, that she would put up a fight about taking medicine. This was not at all the case, in fact it was almost like a weird little game for her sometimes, and she seemed to like it better than formula. It was the "I'm going to let you put this medicine in my mouth, then see how much of it you can shovel back in while I spit it out, then I'll just happily swallow it anyway" game.

It went on this way for a few months without much change. We would take Aliya to her cardiologist, they would do an echo, the doc would read it and consult with us over it, and then the answer would always be the same. The hole hadn't changed much, it was still there and wasn't really getting any better or worse. Each time the doc would say that he wasn't sure yet whether she would need surgery or not, but he was always still hopeful that the hole would close on its own. So we kept giving her the medications, she kept eating like absolute crap, but otherwise was a happy, playful, adorable baby, and we kept chugging forward hoping that the hole would close on it's own. As time grew closer and closer to June, when we knew I would have to go to Fort Hood with my platoon for the month for a training exercise, Mandy and I became increasingly nervous. No matter what neither Mandy or myself, or anyone else for that matter, wanted anything to happen while I was away in Texas.

At a cardiologist appointment in late April we finally got on the road to answers. The doc was going through his usual analysis of the echo and came up with his usual conclusion of "well it's not better and it's not worse." The only difference was that this time he finally followed that up with "I think at this point it would be a really good idea to get her over to Vanderbilt and have a colleague of mine do a heart scope to take a better look." Although we were nervous about what the outcome might be, Mandy and I were both ready to finally get some resolution to this "hole" and finally at least know one way or the other. After a couple of weeks of phone tag, scheduling issues, and juggling, we finally got scheduled in to take Aliya to Vanderbilt to see Dr. P.'s recommended pediatric cardio scope specialist.

We were scheduled to take her for the scope appointment in early May, a month before I was to leave for Texas. When the time came, amidst nervousness and trepidation, we loaded our little girl up in the van and drove her to Vanderbilt Children's hospital for a heart scope.

# Reflections from Hood.

As I am writing this book, it only makes sense that I reflect a little on what everything that is going into it, and the steps that led up to not only the events contained within, but also to me being driven to write about them. So as I write this, I want you as the reader to know that I am doing so from the field at Fort Hood. I brought a small journal notebook out here with me, and I am jotting this down as my thoughts and recollections on these events come to me in between various fire missions and moving around on a mock battle field. I am also doing so unedited, and I intend to type this out for release in a pure and unedited form for all of you that will read it. So it will be real, and it may be flawed...but rest assured the flaws are at least genuine. So spoiler alert, my leaving for Fort Hood will be as far as this book can take you, but don't worry, we still have a lot to cover.

For a little bit of understanding and perspective, I'll fill you in on some back story.

At the time of this writing, I am a soldier in the U.S. Army, specifically the Army National Guard out of Tennessee. For the sake of not getting in trouble over OpSec I won't go into my specific unit, but it's a combined arms heavy brigade. My military job (MOS) is 11c, which just means I am an infantry guy with additional training in mortars. For my part I operate as a member of a heavy mortar platoon, great big 120mm tubes mounted in vehicles.

I joined the Army when I was twenty-five years old (had my twenty-sixth birthday at Fort Benning actually, which sucked big time). By the time I joined up I already had a college degree and a good job, so really my only reasoning was just to serve the country and feel like I was doing a little bit more with my life. You only get one life after all, why not do something with it?

In October of 2011 I went to Fort Benning, Georgia for basic training and infantry school (hence the ring I mentioned in a previous chapter). My experience there was the stereotypical crap-fest you can imagine, if you have ever seen a movie depicting basic training in the military just go ahead and insert that here. Obnoxious drill sergeants (though highly skilled dudes) teaching the skills we needed through a combination of pain and example. Anyone that has been through there can always remember their training unit, and if they can't they are lying to you in one way or another. Mine was first platoon, D company, 1/19th infantry regiment. My "cycle" went through the Christmas holiday, so we "had the privilege" of going home for a couple of weeks right in the middle of training to spend Christmas with our families. This actually was a flat-out terrible idea, as it made the concept of going back to Fort Benning very difficult for most of us...returning to what I call "embracing the suck."

My basic training company also had the distinction of having a tragedy occur about half-way through our cycle.

Basic training in the Army is divided into phases that correspond with how far along in training recruits are, the difficulty and intensity of the training, and types of training they are doing. One of these is called white phase, where privates basically spend all of their time at various ranges learning to shoot. This is called BRM, basic rifle marksmanship, followed up by ARM...you guessed it, advanced rifle marksmanship. All of this just consists of learning basic skills for shooting, and going to a series of ranges to practice before having to shoot a qualifying "table," a test to make sure you can hit a certain number of targets. The culmination of all of it is to shoot at forty targets in various positions (prone, kneeling) for an overall score. Every one of these different rifle ranges was simply designed to improve proficiency with the use of a basic issue weapon, and they were all very strictly controlled when it came to live ammo and firing. Ammo was only handed out to soldiers as they were carefully directed onto a range in small groups, and those coming off of the range would be carefully checked for any remaining live ammo. Apparently Private M. was not checked well enough.

One day at a digital fire range, we were firing at some sort of crazy digital sonar device targets (which would help determine flaws in shooting technique so we could work on them), and we experienced a tragic incident. Most of the shooting day was over and done with, when a young man who I will refer to as Private M. for privacy reasons, was cleared of any ammo and walked off of the range. He walked over to sit on his assault pack, where they were all lined up in neat rows out by the road. We would generally line up our packs out of the way on the very edges away from the ranges in nice, neat rows, and there were plenty of other soldiers who were done for the day sitting over there as well. Private M. went to work on what looked like cleaning his weapon, so no one thought anything of it, but someone should have thought it was odd that he left his helmet on. While sitting there, Private M. removed a single live round from somewhere that he had hidden it, put it directly into the chamber if his M4 (since we could not take magazines off of the range), put the barrel of the weapon under his chin, and pulled the trigger.

The whole range was an immediate circus of confusion and panic, drill sergeants came out of nowhere on all sides to quickly react and get control of the situation. A sergeant named Sanchez was the first on the scene, but there was nothing he could do. The bullet had gone straight up, ricocheted off of the private's helmet, and come back down, doing even more damage. Private M. died right there at the range.

The rest of the day was a blur of medical personnel, cleanup personnel, and high-ranking brass trying to figure out what had just happened. All of us that were there were rounded up under a tin awning on some bleachers, and talked to at length by both our company commander as well as the battalion commander. They went through all of the speeches you would expect about our lives all being precious, and nothing we experienced there being worth doing what he had done. They went on about all of the resources we had, people we could talk to, about their doors always being open, and about how we all needed to be there for each other to prevent stuff like this. They wanted everyone to go and talk to someone else, anyone else, if we were feeling like things were getting close to heading in the remote direction where we might do something like this. None of us were listening very well.

   None of us could believe that one of our own, someone that had been with us for months and experienced the same things that we had experienced, had just shot and killed himself right in the middle amongst us...at the rifle range...at basic training. We all knew that some of us could die, some day, somewhere in combat...but we didn't expect to lose one of our own like that. I didn't know Private M. very well, but it brought a realness to me surrounding everything that we did or experienced for the rest of our time at Fort Benning.

In early March 2012 I walked my tired feet across the field behind the National Infantry Museum, graduated, and left Fort Benning behind.

The six years from then to now in my Army career have been spent with my platoon in TN, with occasional trips to places like Fort Campbell, Camp Shelby, or Fort Hood for various training missions. No deployments, not yet. It has of course had ups and downs, fun times and crap times, times in the field sweating and wearing myself out, just to come home and get used to regular life again (which by the way is actually a really weird and hard thing to do for a National Guard soldier...swapping back and forth between normal civilian life vs. Army life). All in all I had decided along the way that at the end of my six year enlistment that I would go ahead and get out, call six years plenty of time to serve, and walk away.

I only explained all of this to you, the reader, for some perspective on how I got here right now. As I write this at Fort Hood, in the back of a tracked vehicle, I only have about two weeks left on my current enlistment contract. This was supposed to be my last ride, my last hoorah before turning in my gear and waving the Army goodbye. That was all before Aliya...before we knew what kind of medical care she would need, what kind of therapies, and how much I would have to provide her with in order for her to develop and be taken care of. All of that leads to the fact that the day before I left to fly out here I also made a decision to sign a re-enlistment contract with the Army. By the way, based on the increasing intensity of our training schedule and worldwide issues, I am guessing that this decision will land me right in the middle of an overseas deployment in the next one to two years.

All of this is for someone that I just met eight months ago, that I can't even really communicate with properly yet, that costs me big wads of money in food and various things, that keeps me from spending enough quality time with Mandy or doing any number of other things I'd like to be doing. Yet this is already the most amazing little person that I know. She doesn't judge anyone, or stress out about worthless crap, or have any of life's stupid petty little issues. She doesn't have to deal with any of those things, and judging by how she is shaping up right now I don't think she will. Since being here I've received numerous pictures of her (in the few moments I've had enough cell battery to turn my phone on), and those pictures have been the highlight of those days. Seeing her is all I need to keep my morale up and remind me of why I am doing this.

As of right now, this moment, I have been in the field bouncing around from mountain to mountain, mortar firing position to mortar firing position, for ten straight days down here. I haven't showered in those ten days, I've been eating nothing but MREs and crappy field chow, I haven't seen a real latrine/restroom (when you have to dig holes in the woods, bring baby wipes, just a tip), and I've been sleeping on any flat surface I can possibly find. I am caked with sweat and grime, my hair is full of dirt, and I'm covered in heat rash from head to toe. But when I see that little girl smiling at me through a camera, I can't help but smile back. She makes it all worth every moment. I am as happy as can be out here doing this, because I know it's all for her. So that she can have the best life possible, the life that my little girl deserves. When I see her in these pictures that Mandy sends me, I don't see the traces of her condition. I don't see Down Syndrome at all. All I see is a beautiful, happy little girl, looking through the camera at her proud father.

I am sitting on the ground right now finishing up this chapter (I am writing pieces of it in between fire missions), and I can't help but think of the contrast between some of the memories I've described. Between Private M. killing himself, and my daughter's smiling face, she will win and illicit the stronger emotion every time. This is incredible to me.

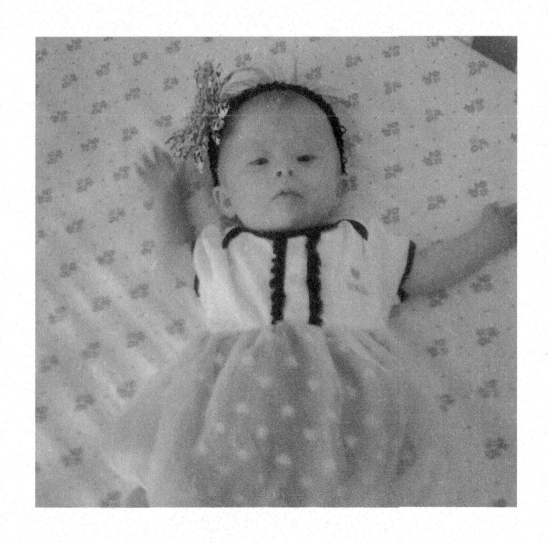

# The Scope.

The children's hospital at Vanderbilt is nothing short of incredible. From the facility itself, to the specialty doctors it attracts, to the top-notch staff. When we arrived the morning of Aliya's heart scope, I was both impressed by the place and at the same time very aggravated by how packed the parking garage was (because of how good the place is).

The heart scope was to be performed there at the children's surgical center, which if I remember right was on the third floor. I remember thinking about how massive the waiting area was for the place, proving that these guys handled a ton of volume in kid's surgeries. The staff was crazy friendly about getting us checked in, they had a clean and smooth process, then we began the waiting period to be called back for prep. This gave me some time to really look around and see how crazy the place was, and I again was just really impressed by something as simple as the layout of a waiting area. When I say waiting area, I mean it was huge. Instead of the typical rows and rows of chairs, they had set up these large half-circle wraparound booths with rows of chairs that closed in the other half of the circle. These booths created a sort of enclosed area that was still open to the rest of the big waiting area, so that larger families would have their own "enclosed" and "separate" type of area to wait together, but still know what was going on and be able to interact with staff as needed. These areas would accommodate probably fifteen people each, and the pediatric surgery waiting area was simply full of them, they were everywhere. I also noticed that the place was covered in signs telling me not to eat or drink anything in there, which seemed really strange to me at first, until I remembered the pre-procedure instructions we had been given for Aliya. From our own instructions I realized that none of the kids in here had been allowed to eat or drink anything, so doing so around them would be incredibly cruel and crappy. There was of course a little area closed off through a door where family member could go if they needed a coke and a snickers, haha.

After a short wait we were called back by a very pleasant nurse, who took Aliya's weight, length, and the rest of her vitals, then put a tag on her ankle for identification. She gave us matching tags for our wrists, so no matter what we could always have access to her while she was there. Once all of that was done, it was time to go back through a big set of double doors to the O.R. prep area. Back there she had her own little cubicle with a crib-bed, and whole team of doctors and nurses swarming in and out going through a battery of pre-op stuff.

For the pre-op they had us put Aliya in a little mini hospital outfit, that despite being a kids XS she was still too small to fill out. It was white with a Vandy Children's logo. Then a nurse came in and re-verified all the important info with us: what is she allergic to? When was the last time that she ate or drank? When was her last diaper rash? What medication was she on? This was all info we had given over and over again, but she double and triple checked all of it anyway. I wasn't annoyed by this, in fact I was happy they were so thorough...when you're baby is in the hospital, thorough is good. Next it was time to meet with the guy performing the scope, Dr. J., and they anesthesiologist, Dr. B. (by the way probably the best anesthesiologist I've ever dealt with). Before we knew it the whole team was assembled there, Dr. B. was getting started with anesthesia, and it was time for us to return to the waiting area so these people could do their jobs. We were ushered back out through those big double doors to the waiting area, left to stew in nervousness until the procedure was complete. The time in the waiting area for that heart scope seemed to be forever, though in reality it was over in less than an hour. That's how awesome these people were.

As soon as the scope procedure was done, but before we could go back and see Aliya, Dr. J. had a short consultation in a side conference room with me to discuss what he had found. He pulled up some pictures and videos on this awesome wall-mounted screen that was linked into a hospital directory for media storage, super awesome and convenient system, to show me the results of the scope. What it showed, and what he explained very conclusively, was that the septal defect she had in her heart was causing her to shunt and pump blood to her lungs at about four times the rate she was supposed to, and less to the rest of her body. What this meant was that she definitely would have to have heart surgery to fix the situation, and it really needed to be sooner rather than later. At that point it was early May, I had to leave for Fort Hood in June, and this thing had to happen. So it either had to be done before I left, or it had to wait until I got back in July...and after conferring on the situation both pediatric cardiologists agreed that they did not want to wait until early July.

Have you ever found out suddenly that your then seven-month-old daughter needed open-heart surgery AND that it had to be done in the next few weeks? Yikes? Wow? Holy crap? Yes, all of the above...especially holy crap.

Once the consultation was done they allowed Mandy and I to go back to recovery and see our daughter. She wasn't really awake yet, but she WAS already sucking down pedialyte like a champ and being a decent sport about the whole thing. She was groggy, sleepy, and a little upset as they started to wake her up, but all in all she was handling it all better than I had expected of her. She never ceases to amaze me with her ability to just handle things as they happen to her. She looked super tiny even in the little kid-sized rolling hospital bed, helpless with all of the monitors and IV hooked up to her once again. She had to stay the night for observation unfortunately, so once she was awake it wasn't very long before they had her wheeled upstairs to a regular room for the night. Mandy was allowed to stay with her, so once again I was going to go home and take care of everything else. Once they were settled in and Aliya was calm, I kissed them both goodbye and I went home for the night.

That night and the next day I let everyone important in Aliya's life know about the outcome of the scope. Some of them had travel plans to make, like my mother, my grandmother, and Mandy's parents. Others just wanted to keep up with what was going on with her, and all of them gave their best wishes for what we were about to undertake. During the course of that next day Aliya came home, happy and radiant as could be. Over the following few days a lot of phone calls were made, but we finally got a date set for surgery. She was set to have the surgery done to correct on May twenty-third, which in theory would have her out of the hospital before I had to leave for Texas...in theory.

# Heart Surgery, and a Baby Girl.

The surgery to fix Aliya's heart was scheduled for a Tuesday, but she had to go in to Vandy the day before to do all of her pre-op testing and make sure that she was ready plus healthy enough to handle surgery. The Sunday prior my mother and grandmother drove up so that they could be there for all of us, and Mandy's parents came up that Monday. Aliya of course had no idea what was going on. All she could tell was that all of these extra people were around and that she was getting tons of attention. She did not act like a baby that needed heart surgery, as I recall, if you looked at her all that you would see was a beautiful little girl with almond eyes, a face full of curiosity (mixed with some confusion), and a ball of barely-contained energy.

The weeks leading up to surgery were some of the best we had ever spent with Aliya. She was getting old enough to start really showing the world what her personality would look like. She rolled around all the time, working on trying to crawl around (though all she could manage was propping up on her elbows and pushing herself around), and she would roll back and forth like a little ninja. She had finally started playing with toys, whatever she could reach and grab. Her grip was actually getting crazy strong for such a little thing. At six to seven months old she only weighed eleven pounds (ish), but she could grab both of my thumbs in her little hands and hold tight enough for me to lift her up out of the crib, off the bed, off the floor, off of the changing table...wherever. We had set up a nice playpen in the main dining room/living room area (open floor plan), a bright thing with soft bottom and sides so we wouldn't have to worry about leaving her in there. It had bright animal designs all over it, and we filled it with every soft toy and stuffed critter we could, so when she was in there she was surrounded by stimulation and things to grab.

This was also the time in Aliya's development when she really started responding to being played with in her own way, with her own personality.

She had always responded by smiling or grabbing my hand, but now she started getting really excited. She made crazy expressive faces, she laughed a ton, and she squirmed with overflowing happiness. We would play this game with her that seemed to be her favorite, along the lines of old-school peek-a-boo. We would cover her eyes for a few seconds, then uncover them suddenly and she would lose her mind with laughter, smiles, and wriggling her whole body with excitement. Mandy also discovered during that time that Aliya loved looking at pictures, especially on a phone. Mandy could show her pictures of me or almost anything on a phone, and Aliya would become mesmerized, then smile that whole-faced smile of hers.

Aliya had always shown signs of being sort of a daddy's girl, but this manifested even more in the time frame between scope and surgery. Sometimes she would be upset, maybe she had been scared by the dogs barking, or woke up scared, or just puked back up some dinner. She would refuse to be calmed down by usual methods, but then sometimes I would pick her up and walk around the house with her, calming her down quickly and usually putting her right to sleep. This was the time period that I made my final decision to re-sign and extend my service with the Army. I knew I had to keep up the insurance; it would keep her able to get the best medical care.

No way could I possible let this happy little girl down.

That Monday before the surgery I had to work (to ensure that I could take time off afterward if needed), so Mandy, my mom and my grandma took her in to Vandy for the pre-op checks. They told afterward that once again the staff had taken her weight, her length, the rest of her vitals, and performed a whole pile of other tests just to make sure that she would be fine to proceed the next day. Everything went fine; she checked out as plenty healthy enough to proceed, so they all came home for the night. A long night.

That night everyone spent as much time as possible with Aliya, which once again she couldn't even comprehend a reason for, but she soaked it up nonetheless. That night I also made sure to update my dad, he wanted to be there for her surgery as well so I had to give him the details in order for him to meet up with us the next morning. I also updated my work, my band, and my friends so everyone would know I would be off the grid the next day or so. Everyone was supportive, as you would expect, and I appreciated every one of them for it.

That Tuesday morning we did not have to have Aliya at the hospital until eleven, so we got her up and ready without having to rush (she was already a little diva in the mornings). Everyone met us there at the house in time to leave (both sets of grandparents and my grandmother), the rest of them following us down to the hospital in sort of a convoy of support. Oddly enough for a Tuesday the traffic in Nashville was light, and the parking garage was not crowded. I took these things as good omens for the struggles of the day ahead.

From the previous visits mentioned earlier in this book, we obviously knew exactly where to go. The surgery was taking place at the same children's surgical area of Vanderbilt as we had been to for the scope and her pre-op testing. We got Aliya checked in, and get up shop in the same huge waiting area with the big sectioned-off family areas, which I was suddenly very glad for and even more impressed by. Between myself, Mandy, my father, my mother, my grandmother, Mandy's mother, and Mandy's step-father, we took up most of one of those sections with enough room to spread out a little. They were all there for support; we needed every bit we could get. Aliya couldn't realize it at the time (she didn't even know she was about to have surgery) but she had a huge extended team behind her at that hospital and outside of it. Everyone else was visibly nervous; I could see them all handling it in their own ways. Grandmothers were knitting, mothers were busying themselves, my father was chain smoking outside and trying to contain his aggravation. The waiting game always sucks.

Thankfully the wait wasn't long before Aliya, Mandy and myself were called back to repeat the same song and dance. Weight, length, vitals...matching ID tags. After that it was through the big double doors once again to surgical prep. By that time most of the team back there were familiar faces, they went over the same precautions with allergies, medications, and gave us the little hospital outfit to put her in. We met with the surgical team, and we got the same anesthesiologist, Dr. B., which I was stoked about because I had specifically requested her again. The actual surgeon performing the procedure was another recommended by our regular pediatric cardiologist, so we trusted he would be the best for the job (since he was doing this at Vanderbilt, it was also a safe bet he was top notch). The surgeon was a polite, soft spoken guy with very sure-looking hands. I will never forget the last thing that I said to him at the end of our pre-operative meeting..."don't screw up."

After the pre-op meetings with our surgical team there was a small window of time before the operation started, so we let the rest of the family take turns coming back to say goodbye before it began. They all did so, and again Aliya was completely confused and blissfully unaware of why any of this was happening. All she knew was she was somewhere weird, and getting lots of attention.

Then the surgical team came back, and it was time to say goodbye to my little girl...trusting her to a team of strangers, specialists in their field...for pediatric heart surgery. I kissed Aliya on the forehead, and they took her back to the operating room.

***

The time spent while Aliya was in surgery was damn-near unbearable for all of us. The procedure was estimated to take around four hours, and it felt more like four years. Dad spent most of the time outside so that he wouldn't go stir-crazy, and grandma went with him for similar reasons. Mandy's parents busied themselves reading or knitting, Mom played on her laptop, and I tried to pass time reading one of Robert Kiyosaki's books (an investment guide if I remember right).

At one point my mother suggested that we go and find something to eat to take our minds off of everything. Mandy refused to leave the waiting area, so I brought her something from Subway. Dad, Mom, Grandma, and myself all decided that Mom's idea was a decent one, so she Googled nearby stuff to eat and chose a little hole-in-the-wall Japanese joint close to the hospital. We wanted to stay close, but leave the actual hospital so we could breathe for a little bit. The place ended up being good, a sushi/hibachi joint with a hot bar for lunch, but nothing could really distract me from the fact that my little girl was on an operating table. During that whole waiting period I was a rock on the surface, a pillar, a solid and unmoving boulder.

Underneath I was a wreck. We ate, we made small talk to pretend everything was fine, and then we went back to the hospital waiting area.

When we got back to the waiting area I tried to do some more reading, again in an attempt to take my mind off of things, and again it didn't work. Everyone was on edge, trying hard to conceal it but it was there regardless. An eternity ticket by in those few hours...one minute at a time. Finally, after what seemed like a century, the nursing staff called us with an update.

It was a quick update; Aliya had done well and was headed for the recovery ICU. Her heart had been suspended and bypassed for a little under an hour while they fixed it. I was told that the ICU would need a good hour or so more to stabilize and get her settled in so that we could go and see her. Once again this seemed like a million friggin' years, just waiting to go up and see her, but at least she was out of surgery and doing well so far.

As soon as was possible we moved everyone up to the ICU waiting room, a much smaller and sterile looking little room with a couple of TVs and some terrible chairs (haha) a couple of floors up from the surgical area. Dad, Mom, and Grandma went ahead and left for the day once they knew she was out of surgery and doing well. The rest of us went up to (I think) the fifth floor, and waited. As we waited I would occasionally go to the front desk there to check on status, and one of those times when I was doing just that I walked up on a scene that I would rather have missed (the waiting area was down a hallway and around a corner from the ICU "reception" desk).

There was a young couple there with what looked like either a couple of family members or friends in tow. The young mother and father were very visibly upset, the mother choking back tears and the guy pacing back and forth with clenched fists (arms covered in tattoo sleeves, wearing an affliction shirt). They were yelling and screaming at the few members of the nursing staff that were present at the desk at that time. From the bits and pieces that I could catch it sounded like their son was in the ICU in critical condition, and because he was not stable they were not allowed back to see him. He was apparently also not expected to make it through the night.

At first I was thinking to myself that even though the situation was direly bad, the young couple was not doing their best to handle it. However as I thought about it more, I tried to imagine myself in their shoes...my child expected to not last the night and me being told that I could not go see her. I decided that if that were the case, the staff would have a much bigger problem on their hands, and I would likely end up in jail. I decided that this young couple had let the staff off easy with just a little yelling, because in that position I imagined that I would likely be throwing things and trying to tear the place apart until I was allowed to see my daughter...or until the cops came, tazed me, and had to drag me away. I felt incredibly terrible for them, could not imagine what they were really going through or feeling (though for me as I said I guessed it would translate into anger). At the same time I was ashamed of myself, because I was selfishly relieved that my daughter so far was doing so well. I felt bad about feeling that way, but I suppose it is only natural and instinctive to do so.

   As a side note that child must have made it through the night. The parents were removed that night by security, but I saw them in passing a few days later when I was headed down the elevators and they were headed for the regular recovery area, so I am guessing (and I hope) that things turned out better for them.

After yet another eternity of waiting, Mandy and I were finally allowed back into the ICU to see Aliya for the first time since surgery. Now that I think about it, Mom and Grandma may have waited to go home until right after being able to see her out of surgery, I can't exactly recall now.

Aliya was in her own little ICU room, and they had her own nurse in there one-on-one with her, which I was thankful for and thought was awesome. The sight of her laying there though just about killed me again. I was incredibly relieved to see her, asleep, breathing, and done with surgery, but I have never seen anything look so helpless in all of my life.

   She was in a normal sized hospital bed, which made her look even smaller, with an oxygen tube in her nose, a tube down her throat, and a mainline IV access in her neck. She was covered in wires, monitors for everything, she had a chest tube in with an open access wound in her side (to drain fluid from her chest cavity), and catheters for waste. She also had an unmistakable scar running from the base of her neck all the way down almost to her belly button. The scar had been sealed over with some sort of crazy medical glue, but no bandages. She also had pacemaker wire access left in, which we were told was a standard procedure on any open-heart surgical patient. The scar had been one of the first things my eyes were drawn to, it was angry looking and a somber reminder of what she had just gone through. The next thing that I noticed, however, brought a smile to my face. In her little right hand, Aliya was squeezing the life out of an empty little tube, like one of the ones that they would used for a blood sample or something. She was still knocked out cold under heavy sedation, but apparently they had put this little tube in her hand for her to squeeze to keep her from yanking the wires and tubes out of everywhere else. Even unconscious, she had been trying to pull out all of the stuff attached to her. This was a tough little miniature woman, definitely stubborn as could be...Daddy's little girl. For a brief moment I pulled the tube out of her hand and let her grab my finger, so maybe somehow subconsciously she would know that I was there.

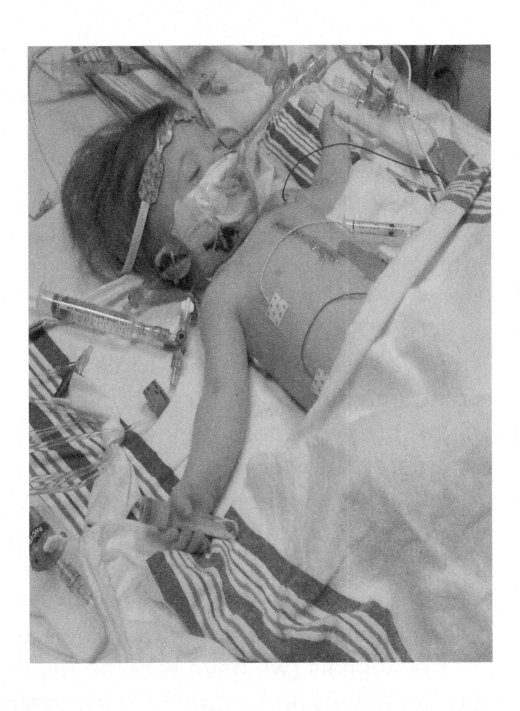

Once I had seen that Aliya was alright with my own eyes, I let the rest of the family go back and see her. They were only allowed back two at a time and not for long, but I figured with all of their waiting and support they at least deserved to lay eyes on her.

The ICU staff was planning to remove the tube from her throat sometime during that first recovery night, but regardless they were ok with one parent staying there in the room with her on a fold out chair-bed thing. Of course I let Mandy stay. I knew that it would be about impossible to pry her out of there anyway, and one of us really needed to go home to take care of the animals (we have way too many between dogs and cats). So once again we decided that she would stay, and I would run back and forth between hospital and home (seems to be one of my better skills...running around taking care of stuff). So I kissed both Mandy and Aliya goodbye for the night, and went home.

As can be expected, the drive home that night was another reflective time. I was thinking back on all of the little things, the subtle nuances that made Aliya who she was becoming. The events of her short life thus far had already been significant, what she had been through that day certainly was, and the inherent strength that she exhibited despite her condition was incredible. All very heavy stuff for a brand new father, but that's what fatherhood is. A series of surprisingly

heavy things, and learning to love
every moment.

# Recovery.

Aliya was out of the ICU in a day and was put into her own recovery room with Mandy, up one more floor from the recovery ICU. She was all the way in the back corner of the main pediatric recovery area, actually only one room over from a recovery room that she had used previously (after the scope).

Mandy's parents stayed for a couple of days after the surgery before heading back down to Florida, my mother and grandmother ended up staying for most of the hospital recovery time (Mom had to get back to Florida a day or two prior to Aliya being released so she could go back to work, she is an E.R. charge nurse). So the fact that I needed to keep running back and forth between the hospital, home, and work ended up not being a big deal, because that hospital room stayed full of visitors during pretty much all visiting hours. I would go and see her in the mornings, then go to work all day, and then go see her again in the evenings before heading home to let the dogs out and all of that nonsense. It made for long days, but I was so stoked about Aliya's recovery and how well it was going that I didn't even care.

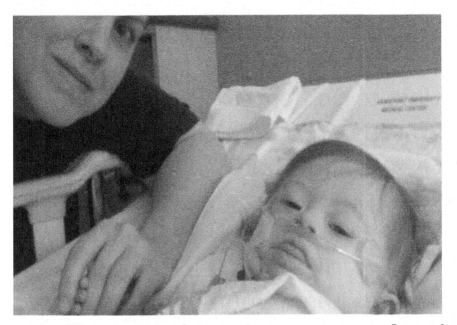

She was there in recovery for the better part of a week. Each day she would get a little bit better, a little bit more alert and playful (which I really had to be careful of with two large areas on her upper body healing, unfortunately her father is not known for being gentle), and each day a few more wires or tubes would be taken off of her. She looked more and more like a normal baby and less like a cyborg, until one day finally everything came off, and we got our little girl back. It was time to go home! While we had been there in recovery we had a visit from a couple of the Down's network people again, just to offer support and feed us dinner, which was awesome and very much appreciated (great people, look them up in your area if you have a child with Down's).

Of course the recovery process didn't end the moment we got home, but everyone was very thankful to have Aliya out of the hospital. Those first few days at home it was all anyone could do to keep her from rolling over on her stomach, which prior to surgery was one of her favorite pass-times. She loved to be on her belly, loved to play on her belly, loved trying (not successfully yet) to crawl around, and worst of all for the recovery process she loved to SLEEP on her belly. The biggest problem with all of this was that the number one, most important, don't-break-it piece of instruction that we had been give for her recovery of course was...that she was absolutely not allowed to be on her stomach for several weeks following surgery. She had to avoid any pressure or damage to the opening on her chest. Needless to say that my daughter was not very impressed by this notion at all, and did her very best to run all of us ragged trying to keep up with keeping her on her back. I almost think that she somehow knew what was up and had decided to make it into a little game of her own. "Let's see how many time I can make them run over here and flip me back over" was the name of the game...and the answer was "a lot."

As the days ticked by, Aliya got better and better, more and more back to "normal." Whatever you could define "normal" as an energetic and curious baby with Down Syndrome anyway. That also meant that the days were getting closer to my leaving for Texas (she was only released from Vandy about five days prior to my scheduled flight out with my boys), so time was short to spend with her and make sure that she was really healthy enough before I left. All in all it was time spent as best as I could, and I was happy to at least get that. We had arranged for my grandmother to stay with Mandy and Aliya during my absence, so I knew that the three of them would be ok, they could hold it all together while I was gone.

On the morning of June 4th I put all of my gear in the truck, kissed everyone goodbye (Aliya especially), and drove to the armory to wait for the flight to Fort Hood.

# Father's Day.

It is now Sunday, June eighteenth, Father's day...and here we sit at Fort Hood. This seems to be a recurring theme with the Army, somehow every single Father's day we are out training somewhere...generally somewhere hot and sticky...instead of being able to spend time with our families. Of course in previous years this never mattered to me at all...in fact I criticized the other guys for being babies about it. Aliya is my first child, and at this time last year she was just a little blip on an ultrasound screen, so it hadn't seemed real yet.

With all that we've been through together up to this point, it feels real enough now. Using power inverters hooked into military vehicles that they weren't made to work with, we all found ways to charge our cell phones enough to turn them on (they've been dead or close to it since we got here), and we all contacted our dads for Father's day. When I did this I received a picture from Mandy where she had dressed Aliya up in a "Happy Father's day" onesie thing that also had her name on it. Made a crap day better, so thank you baby.

This platoon of mine is filled with fathers, so at least I'm in the middle of nowhere with a bunch of other guys who are all in the same boat. Among just my platoon we have myself, Lyons, Jacobs, Townsend, Brisco, Coomer, Carrasco, Short, Williams, Ski, Tallman, Ryan, Hines,

Zimmerlee...and I'm sure I'm missing someone else...all fathers. In fact there are very few men in this outfit that are NOT fathers.

We all know what we are out here for though. We are out here running missions on father's day so that our kids can have decent futures, so it's all good.

# More from Hood.

Now that we are past the part where Aliya had he heart surgery and her (thankfully) quick road to recovery, we can fast forward back to present for a few minutes and rejoin me at Fort Hood (after the Father's day thoughts). It's Monday the nineteenth of June, and supposedly we are nearing the end of this field mission. Tomorrow is supposed to be some sort of massive battalion maneuver before we head back to the rear to turn in the gear (always my favorite sign that it's close to go-home time), but today has been a low-key day. Not many fire missions have been called in, so we have had some time to play a couple rounds of spades, catch up on needed sleep, and some of us even watched Hacksaw Ridge on a phone that had just enough battery left.

It's come high time in the writing of this book that I start drawing some conclusions, making a point, telling the reader (whoever that may be if I ever publish this in the first place, and if anyone picks it up to read it) what I am really trying to say here. Unfortunately for you, the reader, I decided that I'm the one writing this thing, so if I want to take another moment for a little more perspective, then so be it.

The last couple of days, as our battalion does better and better in these mock-combat scenarios (which we are getting scored on by a special group of regular Army cadre called

OCs) we have been hearing, like we always do, that this unit is likely to deploy within the next couple of years. The latest theory is that it could be as early as next year, and may even be to the border of Poland (the border it shares with Russia). Apparently the Army has been rotating heavy brigades in and out of there, and we just happen to be a heavy brigade combat team. Hooray for us! The point of all of this being that I may in the near future have to spend a significant amount of time away from Mandy, and from the little girl that I've written so much about in the dirty pages of this notebook (can't keep anything clean out here...). That thought isn't much fun to me, let alone having to leave the rest of my friends, family, work, music, bands, and everything else all behind to go play with Putin for a while. But hey, if I have to go, then I'll go with a smile on my face.

# Reflections.

June 22nd, 2017, Fort Hood. We came back in from the field yesterday, all of us, the whole brigade full of us. It was an absolute mess to be perfectly honest with you, several thousand soldiers all coming back in at once, scrambling to clean and turn in vehicles, weapons, equipment, and all funneling through the same small places to do it. We keep our personal weapons with us of course until we get home to Nashville, but everything else has to be turned in. It was a complete cluster grenade all day yesterday, but we got it done, and now we are just chilling out in a huge military tent city just outside main post, waiting for our flights or buses home on Saturday (the

24th). Unless of course they get delayed by this tropical storm that's rolling in...but we can cross that bridge IF we get to it.

That means that I have some time to kick back on a cot (yes, a cot! You know you have been sleeping in some pretty crappy places when a cot excites you) and write to you some more, whoever you may be. Lucky you, haha.

So when I started writing this thing I wasn't even settled on what to write about, much less whether or not I would finish it. I definitely didn't know if I would bother publishing it, but I have felt the need to finish a book for a while now. I've started a couple of fictional pieces over the years but never had the passion to finish them. The problem has always been that I didn't have a topic that I felt strongly enough about to finish it. Obviously if you've read this far, you know that I have found that topic, and her name is Aliya. I sat down and wrote the draft for this book in a hardback notebook journal, a few lines at a time in between missions, during the twenty days of XCTC training evaluations at Fort Hood, Texas. Of course if you read this far you already picked up on that though.

As you no doubt have gathered from the previous chapters, my daughter's name is Aliya (pronounced Ah-lee-uh), and she was born with an extra chromosome called Trisomy 21, a condition more commonly known as Down Syndrome. She was my first child, and at the time of this writing in

June 2017 she is my only child. I'm that guy who never thought he would have kids in the first place, I was always too on the move for it, too busy living life and doing way too many things at once. Now that I have her I would not give her back for the whole world. I'm sure that any decent father would say the same about his child, not sure how many would really mean it, but I'm not in the habit of saying things just to say things.

When I first learned that I would be a father, I wasn't sure what to really think of it. I wasn't sure whether to be happy or depressed, excited or scared. I was reasonably sure that I could pull off being a decent father because I've been looking after people for most of my life, spent a lot of my early life helping to take care of my two brothers with a single Mom that worked all the time, and have managed enough people in my professional life that I end up feeling like a father anyway. What I wasn't sure of was whether or not I really WANTED to be a father. The answer turned out to be a resounding yes, but Aliya had to show me the way to that answer, she had to show me that I did.

When Mandy and I first found out about Aliya's condition, we of course were a little upset about it, scared, and uncertain about how it would change our lives. I wrote previously in this book about the choice that I had to make as to whether or not she would even be born at all. Obviously I decided she would, and we as a result

(Mandy and I together) decided that she would. No matter what else was true, she was mine, and MY child deserved a chance. So we gave her one, and she has proved from day one that she deserved it. She's also been through a lot more in her first eight months than any child should have to go through, but that's the way the cards fell, and she has handled it like an absolute champ.

My little girl will likely be small her entire life. At eight months old she is about twelve and half pounds of pure wriggling tornado. She has her father's reddish-brown hair, light blue eyes (though hers are decidedly more almond-shaped), and reddish eyebrows. Thankfully she got the rest of her looks from her mother (brownie points?). She's a beautiful little girl, and when she looks at you with that quizzical little smirk, she will melt you from the inside out.

Aliya does not know that she has Down Syndrome. She has no idea that the world expects her to be different, delayed, or slow. She doesn't know that she will look a little different than your "standard" (whatever that means) person. She doesn't know that the world will try to hold her back because of her condition. She also doesn't know (YET) that the world and everyone in it will have to deal with her father if they stand in her way. She doesn't need to know any of these things yet, and many of them she may never need to. All that she knows and all that matters are the facts that she is here, her mother and father love her, and she is for the most part a very happy baby. At this point she is not even aware of the medical problems that she has had. She doesn't know about the procedures we've taken her in for, the hospitals, or any of that. She knows that she has awakened sometimes and hasn't felt so good...she has been sore from time to time, but she didn't know why. Again all she knows is that she's here, people love her, and she is figuring the world out. I decided very early on that she was very lucky in the way that she is learning to view the world, with a clean and unassuming mind.

When Aliya was born I also made a decision not to coddle her anymore as a result of her having Down's then I would if she had been born without it. Don't get me wrong, she is daddy's little girl, and I will literally tear the whole world apart to protect her, but I'm not going to treat her as if anything is wrong with her, because from both of our perspectives there isn't. There may be certain things she will not be able to do or master, like flying a plane...but I am going to let her find her own limits. I'm not going to let the world tell her that she can't do something just because she has an extra chromosome. I will push her to do the most and be the best that she possibly can, and I'll do whatever she needs of me in order to help her achieve her goals. That's my promise to her.

We have already begun having her evaluated so if she needs any therapies we can make those happen as early as possible. Most kids with Down's need at least some form of therapy (some need much more than others), be it physical, occupational, speech, or any other form. We will not know until she is a little older if she will need speech (she does already babble and try to talk quite a bit), but they can start on some of the others very soon if she needs them.

# Advice.

    As a fairly new dad myself and definitely a newcomer to the my-kid-has-Down-Syndrome club, I know that it can be a difficult and somewhat scary pill to swallow at first. There are a few pieces of advice, however, that I can offer up, most of them being mental/internal, and all of them being purely from my own perspective. That being said, take them at face value for what they are worth, and adapt to your own needs.

    First of all, go home and enjoy your baby. Just go with it and don't miss out on what is an awesome time to be alive, and to be a parent. This was something that a lady from the Down's support network said to me off-the-cuff during that first welcome visit at the hospital when Aliya was born, and for some reason it stuck. It was true. It was real. I had asked the woman a question about what we should expect, what did we need to know, what did we need to do when we got home? She simply told me to go home, and enjoy the baby. She said that the rest of it could come later, and we could handle it as it came. So we took our baby home, and this ended up being crazy true. Aside from obvious medical side issues that can arise, the first few months with a Down Syndrome baby are not all that much different than the first few months with any baby, at least in MOST cases. They may show a couple of little quirks, but for the most part they are just babies, Feed them, let them sleep, play with them, love them, and they won't disappoint you. All the rest of it, the therapy, the learning obstacles, and the whole bag of Down Syndrome challenges can wait a little while. They will come, so handle them as best you can when they do, and you will be fine. For now just go home, and enjoy your child.

Secondly, get a little bit of education on what Down's REALLY is and the affects it can actually have on your family. I myself was amazed at how varied the symptoms and effects of the condition really can be. It varies greatly in how it manifests itself in different kids, and to what degree.

Some kids with Down's have issues with speech but are physically well coordinated, while others speak fine but need physical therapy. Some need neither of these, but have other medical issues or need social and occupational therapies. For example if you have read this far you know that my daughter had a heart defect and needed early surgery (a month prior to writing this page). What I may not have mentioned was that she will start some basic occupational therapies soon as well. Other Down's kids we have met needed multiple surgeries, some needed none. Most states have a local Down Syndrome support network, get involved with them, learn what others can teach you, they are a great resource and tool for education as well as support. These people have been here and done this, and they can make your life a little easier by giving you a head start on the learning curve, take it. Read a few good books on Down's, if you are reading this book then this idea must have already occurred to you (unless I know you personally, in which case thanks for the support). This book was not intended to be about Down Syndrome itself, but rather my daughter's journey so far with it. There are plenty of great books out there already about the condition, and your local Down's network can recommend them to you!

Third, and this one is important, BE SUPPORTIVE AND PATIENT. These things need to go hand in hand. Your kids will always need support, kids with

Down's may need it a little more, so give it to them. You can't afford to have a bad day, you need to be your best and give your best for them so that they can do it for you. Give them the tools that they need to be the best people that they possibly can become, the wonderful people that we know they can grow into. At the same time be patient with them, your kid with Down's may take longer to master certain things, that's fine. Just be patient, teach them, and give them what they need. They may just surprise you. These kids will give you so much more than you give them if you let them; they have advantages over all of us in the way that they tend to view the world, free from the petty issues that plague most of us. You owe it to a kid with Down's, as you do with any child, to help them be all that they can be while also having the patience to let them do just that.

***

Take a moment for yourself, and just breathe. I decided to write this book for a couple of reasons. First off I am absolutely crazy head-over-heels nuts about my daughter. She's the light in my eyes, and the fuel that I need to accomplish almost anything difficult that I decide to tackle.

On top of that, not to state the obvious...but Aliya has Down Syndrome. You, the reader, are well aware of this by now. She was born with Trisomy 21 and has had some challengers thus far in her life, so I felt that someone else out there might want to read about her story, and gain any value they possibly could from it. I knew that there would be other people out there going through the same things, or had already gone through them and maybe those people would want to know that they were not alone.

For people to connect on these types of topics I think is very important, because some people have differing levels of resilience, and to know that you are not alone in your struggle may be all that you really need to pick yourself up by your shoelaces and move forward. One step at a time. Maybe you already knew everything in this book and my words have not helped you, that's fine too, maybe all you got out of this was the entertainment value from the story. If so that's awesome too, and I'd like to thank you personally for picking up my book...AND making it to the end.

In any case just remember that if you have a child with Down Syndrome you have been blessed, not cursed. You will face challenges...life is full of those anyway, no denying it. Those challenges will also make you stronger and more fulfilled if you can get your mind in the right place. You have been given one massive opportunity to make a difference in this world. You have the opportunity to raise and know one of the most beautiful people you'll ever meet. Congrats, don't waste it!

Thank you all so very much for reading this book.

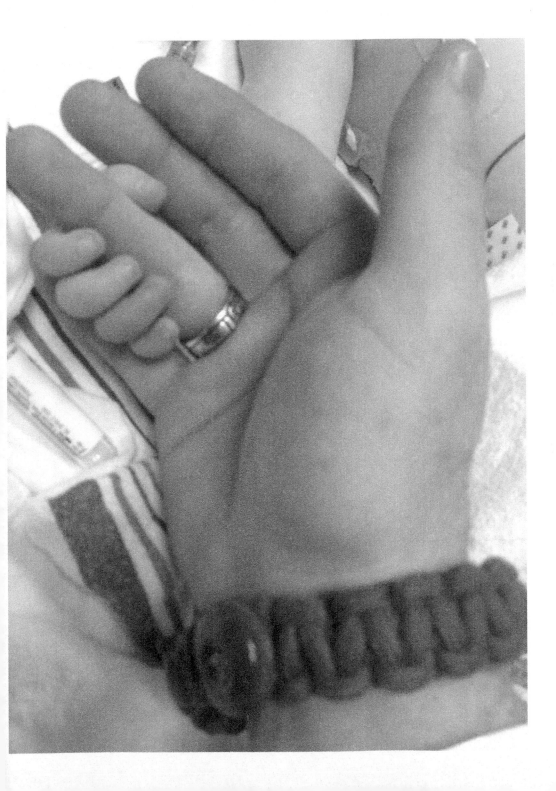

Thank you so much to everyone who made it possible for me to write this book. And thank you to anyone who took the time to read it. Though it may seem like such a small thing, just the ability to write, publish, and share this with the world means a lot to me, and has been the best kind of therapy a father could ask for.

If you have any questions, comments, or need anything at all do not hesitate to contact me. Let's have a conversation about it. I am becoming more and more interested in reaching out to motivate the world around me, and help anyone in any way possible, or get help FROM them. I will include some ways to reach me on the next page.

# Reach out to me:

thealexsimmons.com

www.instagram.com/thealexsimmons

www.facebook.com/alexander.simmon
s1

www.youtube.com/channel/UCAyZgb7
0cLjvQy77ETwj35A

asimmons11c@gmail.com


Find me. Reach out. Let's have a
conversation.